OFF TO GOA

SONIA MEHTA

PUFFIN BOOKS
An imprint of Penguin Random House

PUFFIN BOOKS

USA | Canada | UK | Ireland | Australia | New Zealand | India | South Africa | China | Singapore

Puffin Books is part of the Penguin Random House group of companies whose addresses can be found at global.penguinrandomhouse.com

Published by Penguin Random House India Pvt. Ltd
4th Floor, Capital Tower 1, MG Road,
Gurugram 122 002, Haryana, India

First published in Puffin Books by Penguin Random House India 2017

Picture Credits
P 7: Ferry (Nataliia Sokolovska/Shutterstock.com); P 13: Ruby-throated yellow bulbul (© Gururaj), matti tree (© dinesh_valke [CC BY-SA 2.0 (https://creativecommons.org/licenses/by-sa/2.0/deed.en_GB)], via Flickr); P 18: St Francis Xavier stain glass (Zvonimir Atletic/Shutterstock. com); P 26: Men dancing (Radiokafka/Shutterstock.com); Women with flowers (Radiokafka/Shutterstock.com); P 27: Men in a yellow car (Radiokafka/Shutterstock.com); King Momo at the carnival (GSK919/Shutterstock.com), Men dressed as clowns (joviton dcosta/Shutterstock. com); P 36: Church of Our Lady of the Rock of France (© Bhavna Sinha); P 37: St Francis Xavier statue (Murgermari/Shutterstock.com); P 42: Boats on the beach (Olga Vasilyeva/Shutterstock.com); Men on a fishing boat (Mishakov Valery/Shutterstock.com)

The views and opinions expressed in this book are the author's own and the facts are as reported by her, which have been verified to the extent possible, and the publishers are not in any way liable for the same.

The information in this book is based on research from bonafide sites and published books and is true to the best of the author's knowledge at the time of going to print. Conversations have been created to enliven and narrate the story and are not verbatim utterances. The author is not liable for any further changes or development in incidents occurring post the publication of this book.

ISBN 9780143440741

Design and layout by Quadrum Solutions Pvt. Ltd
Printed at Repro India Limited

www.penguin.co.in

This is a legitimate digitally printed version of the book and therefore might not have certain extra finishing on the cover.

Hello Kids!

I'm so happy you are reading this book. India is an incredible country and there are lots of things about it that we never get to hear about.

I discovered India because my father was in the Indian army. He was posted to many places all over India—and we dutifully followed him. Can you imagine that by the time I was in the tenth standard, I had changed nine schools? Of course it was hard making new friends almost every year, but the good part was that I got to live in so many places. Right from Kerala, where I was born, to Kashmir, Jhansi, Shillong, Chandigarh, Goa . . . the list is long.

Every time I go to a new place, I feel amazed at how different each state is from the other—and yet, how similar. Did you know that we can see monuments from the Stone Age right here in India? Or that we have more than twenty official languages, and most Indians know three or four on an average? Or even that some of the world's most amazing scientific marvels were invented in India?

Oh, there are many, many, many fun and fantastic things about the states of India, which we simply must get to know.

So get your backpack ready, get set to meet some new friends, and join me on a fun trip as we DISCOVER INDIA, STATE BY STATE.

I hope you enjoy reading this book as much as I have enjoyed writing it. I would love to hear from you. So do write to me at sonia.mehta@quadrumltd.com.

Lots of love,
Sonia Aunty

Mishki and Pushka have come to visit Earth from their home planet, Zoomba. They have never seen such an amazing place. Zoomba doesn't have trees and mountains and rivers like Earth does. But the people look exactly the same. When they come to Earth, they meet a sweet old man whom they call Daadu Dolma. Daadu Dolma shows them all the wonderful places in India and tells Mishki and Pushka all about them.

Mishki and Pushka can't believe what they see. They have seen a lot of Earth, but they have never, ever seen a place like India.

They are off to explore India state by state :)

Mishki

Mishki is a curious little girl. She is always asking loads of questions. On her home planet, she is always getting into trouble for poking her nose into things that are not her business.

Pushka

Pushka is Mishki's brother. He loves adventure. He is always ready for a new challenge. Whether it's climbing a mountain, or diving into a cold, cold sea, he is up for it.

Daadu Dolma

Daadu Dolma is a wise old man who has lived on Earth longer than the mountains and the seas. No one knows quite how old he is, but he certainly has been around. He knows everything about everything.

Mishki and Pushka are very excited. They have heard so much about the beach and sea and the yummy food you get in Goa.

'I can't wait to get going,' says Mishki.

'Make sure you have packed your spade and bucket,' says Pushka.
'We will make lots of sandcastles and play on the sand.'

'Oh, but I want to see much more than the beaches,' says Mishki. 'I have heard there are lovely churches and temples in Goa. We must see it all.'

'Yes, of course,' agrees Daadu Dolma. 'No visit to Goa is complete without its churches and temples.'

And so, Mishki and Pushka are ready for their Goan adventure. They are

OFF TO GOA!!!

A SNEAK PEEK

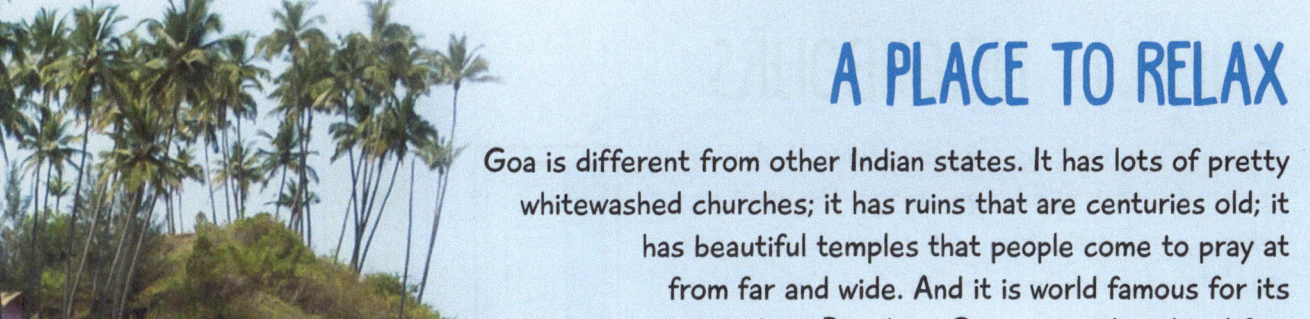

A PLACE TO RELAX

Goa is different from other Indian states. It has lots of pretty whitewashed churches; it has ruins that are centuries old; it has beautiful temples that people come to pray at from far and wide. And it is world famous for its beaches. People in Goa seem relaxed and fun.

RIVER FACT

There are nine main rivers that criss-cross Goa. Some of them are the Mandovi, Zuari, Terekhol, Chapora, Kushavati and Sal. These rivers are full of activity. There are ferries that carry people and cars; there are barges that carry mineral and iron ore; there are pleasure boats with people singing and dancing. Oh, the rivers of Goa are a wonderful sight.

Cars onboard!

CREEKS AND ESTUARIES AND TINY BEACHES

Because of its rivers popping out into the sea from various points, and because they weave in and out of the land, they form lots of creeks and estuaries. These create cosy little pockets for fishermen to safely keep their boats when they are not using them.

FRIENDLY NEIGHBOURS

Goa has a long, long, long coastline. It shares its border with two Indian states. Do you know which ones? Well, if you don't, here goes. Goa has Maharashtra to its north. And Karnataka to its south. On its eastern side are the Western Ghats and of course, on its west, the Arabian Sea.

Maharashtra

Karnataka

Goa

The Old Customs House in Panaji. Looks lovely, doesn't it?

मडगाँव जं
मडगाँव जं - MADGAON

NORTH AND SOUTH

Goa is divided into two main regions—North Goa and South Goa. Panaji (also known as Panjim) is the main headquarters of North Goa, while Madgaon is the main headquarters of South Goa. Panaji is the capital of Goa.

Some of the other important cities that you will hear of when you visit Goa are Vasco da Gama, Mapusa and Ponda.

RED RED MUD

Mud + iron ore

Goa is very different from other states. Look, its mud is red! Do you know why? Because it is full of iron ore and other minerals. Mmmmm! The red mud smells lovely, doesn't it? Did you know that iron and manganese ore are among Goa's largest exports?

MIXED-UP RIVERS

Pushka has forgotten the names of the rivers of Goa. But the names are all jumbled up. Can you un-jumble them so he remembers?

I V O M D A N _____

R I A U Z _____

O L H K R E E T _____

A V I T H S U K A _____

L A S _____

Mishki, put on your hat. It's so sunny!

Oh yes! Goa can get very hot, all right.

Summer in Goa can be hot, hot, hot. In fact, summer is at its hottest in the month of May.

Ouch!

WEATHER VANE

Goa has a tropical monsoon climate. Which means it is hot and humid most of the year. But when it rains!!! Ah! Goa becomes magical in the rains. It rains and rains from June to September. The south-west monsoon arrives in June and the skies open up. The fields turn every shade of green, coconut palms sway and the sky has shades of pink and orange and blue and grey.

January and February are the coldest months.

SUMMER TIME IS MANGO TIME

Yes, indeed! Say summer and you think of mangoes. Goa grows the most amazing types. Mancurado and Hilario are the local favourites. You must try them if you visit Goa in summer.

Did you know? There are eighty-two types of mangoes grown in Goa. Yummmm!

Do It Yourself
Mango Porcupine

It's mango season. So Daadu Dolma is teaching Mishki and Pushka how to make a mango porcupine that they can eat. You can try it too!

1 Cut a slice of mango as shown.

2 Cut it criss-cross into tiny cubes.

3 Bend the mango slice outward. It will be shaped like the back of a porcupine.

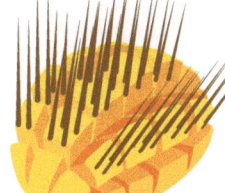

4 Add toothpicks to make the prickly spikes.

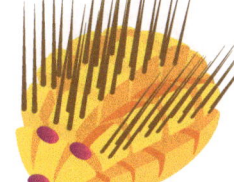

5 Add Gems to make eyes and nose.

Your mango porcupine is ready!

Look at these tall trees! Do you know what they are?

COCONUT TREES!!!

FOREST FANTASY

A large part of eastern Goa is covered by the Western Ghats. This hilly area is thick with forests that are home to some amazing birds and animals. In fact, some travellers have compared Goa's forests to the Amazon and Congo forests for their biodiversity (which means the different kinds of birds and animals that are found there).

There are more than 275 species of birds in these forests; nearly fifty kinds of animals and over sixty types of reptiles.

Wow! Isn't that amazing?

COCO-MANIA

Everywhere you look, there are tall coconut trees swaying in the wind. Which is why Goans cultivate coconuts. They sell a lot of things made from them. You will also see vast green plantations growing paddy and rice. Because it has such a large coastline, there are lots of fisheries everywhere across Goa.

FUN FACTS

Cash crops
Coconut, areca nut cashewnut, banana, sugar cane, pineapple and mango

State animal
Gaur

State bird
Ruby-throated yellow bulbul

State tree
Matti

Do It Yourself
Coconut Toons

Did you know that coconuts have faces? Look at how Pushka has made this amazing face using a coconut shell. Ask your mother for an empty coconut shell and paint it to make a coconut face like Pushka!

Long, long ago

Daadu Dolma, how old must Goa be? It looks very young to me.

Oh no, no! Goa is mentioned in some very, very old scriptures as far back as when the Mahabharata was written. That is almost in 1000-500 BCE.

In those days, it used to be called Gomantak, which in Sanskrit means 'fertile land'. It was also called Gove or Gowapura. It became Goa only when the Portuguese arrived many, many years later.

 Gomantak ▸ Gowapura ▸ Goa

WHERE DID GOANS COME FROM?

In the Vedic period, the river Saraswati, which is in North India, dried up. The people who lived around the river went looking for newer places to move to where they could farm land. One lot of Brahmins moved to Goa. They were called Goud Saraswat Brahmins (from the river Saraswati). They were the first settlers in Goa.

LORD PARSHURAM'S ARROW

A legend goes that one day Lord Parshuram went up the Western Ghats. From there he shot an arrow into the sea and commanded Lord Samudra (Sea God) to leave that place. The place where the arrow fell became a famous beach called Benaulim (from the word benali, meaning arrow).

WOW! THAT'S REALLY OLD!

Goa was actually a part of the Mauryan empire. For over 1000 years, different Hindu kings and dynasties ruled over Goa. Each of them built their own temples and forts. There were the Satavahanas of Kolhapur, the Kadambas and the Chalukyas. Then the Muslims attacked. But they didn't like the beach and sea too much, so they soon left Goa. For some time, the Vijaynagar Empire ruled Goa.

When the Portuguese arrived, they changed Goa forever.

Time to Sketch

Look at how people dressed in Goa a long time ago. Can you redraw this man?

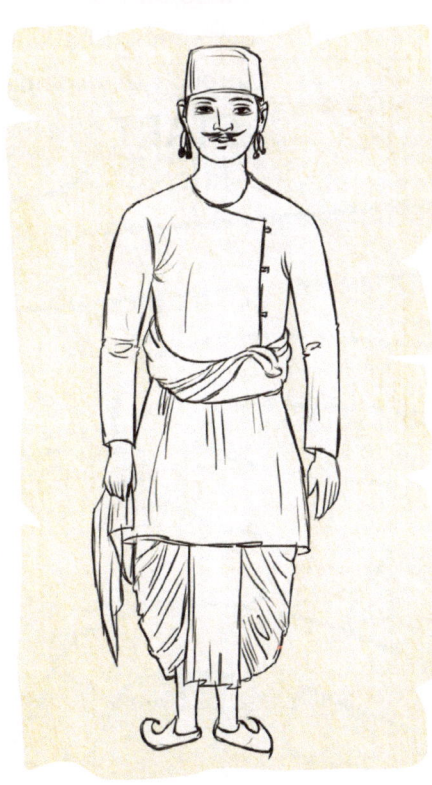

Draw here

VASCO DA GAMA ARRIVES

Vasco da Gama was a restless Portuguese explorer who had set out to explore the world. The Portuguese were looking for a port in India that they could use for trading. Goa was perfect. Vasco da Gama landed in India. Soon, the Portuguese spread out and established a colony here.

For over 450 years, the Portuguese ruled over Goa.

LOST ??

Vasco da Gama needs to find his way to Goa but seems lost. Can you help him find his way through this complicated sea route?

START
HERE

A NEW WAY OF LIFE

The Portuguese began to convert the local people to Christianity. Many Portuguese married Indian women. And soon Portuguese culture crept into the Goan way of life.

The Portuguese brought with them new ways to cook food, wear clothes and celebrate festivals. Many local people began to speak Portuguese. That's why people have Portuguese surnames, like D'Souza, D'Silva, Cabral and Albuquerque.

Did you know?
There is a city in Goa named after Vasco da Gama.

ROME OF THE EAST

For many years, the Portuguese did a lot of good things for Goa. They built beautiful churches and houses. They made the local population quite rich because they were such clever traders. They built so many churches that Goa was called Rome of the East!

Goa

It looks like it was an interesting time. So much happening.

Yes, indeed. Goa has a very interesting history.

HERE COMES THE CHURCH

The Portuguese brought their religion along with them. The king of Spain was worried that the Portuguese who settled in Goa would forget their roots and their religion. So he sent St Francis Xavier to Goa—to remind the Portuguese of their religion and also to convert as many people as possible to Christianity.

THE MIRACLE OF ST FRANCIS XAVIER

St Francis Xavier spent many years in and around Goa. He taught children, he preached in churches and he spread the word of Jesus Christ. People loved him. When he died, his body was kept in a silver casket in the Basilica of Bom Jesus in Old Goa. Every ten years, people came to see his body on his birth anniversary. People believed that by touching his body, illnesses would be cured. The body is not on display any more.

St Francis Xavier's body was on display for over 400 years.

NEWS

FIGHT FOR INDEPENDENCE

All through the Portuguese rule, the local people tried to get their independence back. The fight for Indian independence from the British was going on. In 1947, India became independent, but the Portuguese refused to leave.

Pandit Nehru, who was the Prime Minister of India, ordered an invasion on the Portuguese in Goa. There were 30,000 Indian troops and only 3000 Portuguese soldiers. The Portuguese gave up and finally, after 450 years, Goa was free.

What a battle it must have been!!

A NEW STATE IS BORN

Although the Portuguese left, now there was a new fight. Some Goans wanted Goa to be a separate area called a Union Territory. And others wanted Goa to merge with India and become a state. People voted, and finally, one day in May 1987, Goa became India's twenty-fifth state.

CRACK THE CODE

Can you crack this important message that Pushka and Mishki are trying to decipher?

G = 1	O = 2	A = 3	I = 4	S = 5	N = 6
W = 7	S = 8	W = 7	S = 8	T = 9	E = 10

1 2 3   4 5   6 2 7   3   8 9 3 9 10.

___ ___ ___   ___ ___   ___ ___ ___   ___   ___ ___ ___ ___ ___.

- How are you? = Tu kashi asa? (for a girl)
- How are you? = Tu kosso asa? (for a boy)
- What is your name? = Tumche nau kitay?
- My name is Mishki. = Majay nau Mishki.
- Please = Por favor (Portuguese)
- Thank you = Obrigaado (Portuguese)
- Child = Chardu
- I want = Maka zai
- I don't want = Maka naka
- Where = Khayee
- Up/Down = Vair/Sakail
- Come/Go = Yo/Vas
- Water = Udak

Did you know?
The Goan way of life is often defined by the Portuguese word 'susegaad', which means to chill.

MATCH THE WORDS

Now, can you match these words to their Konkani or Portuguese meanings?

| Where | Child | I want | I don't want | Come | Thank you | Water | Up |

| Vair | Maka zai | Yo | Udak | Obrigaado | Chardu | Khayee | Maka naka |

A peep into their life

Daadu Dolma, look! There are so many people doing so many types of dances.

Yes, dancing is an important part of Goan culture. Come, let me tell you about it.

DANCE DANCE DANCE

Goan culture is bright and different from many other parts of India. That is because, over hundreds of years, different people came to Goa, lived there and left behind a little bit of their lifestyle. People say that Goans are born with music and football in their blood.

KUNBI

This is the most famous dance. The Kunbi tribe performs this dance. Men and women stand in rows and dance. The fisherfolk love to do this.

FUGDI

Women get together and do this dance. There are no instruments but there are special fugdi songs that women sing as they dance.

CORREDINHO

This a Portuguese folk dance that the Goans love to perform during weddings and festivals.

DHALO

Women dance on moonlit nights for a week-long festival. They offer prayers to Mother Earth to protect their households.

SHADOWPLAY

Can you find the shadow of Daadu Dolma? He seems to have lost it.

DHANGAR

The shepherd community does this dance. Mostly men perform it during the festival of Navratri.

That's interesting. I would like to try it someday.

Shigmo celebration

FESTIVE TIME

It feels as if the Goans are always celebrating! There are many festivals that are celebrated in a big, big way. Ganesh Chaturthi, Diwali, Christmas, Easter, Padvo, Shigmo, the Feast of St Francis Xavier—all these are celebrated with gusto. Food, music, dance and prayer—everything is done with lots of fun and games.

Did you know?
Shigmo is celebrated to honour warriors when they came home after battling with the Portuguese.

CARNIVAL CRAZE

It's time for the greatest party ever. It's time for the Carnival! The Goa Carnival is celebrated in February every year and everybody seems to go completely crazy!

IT'S PARTY TIME

For three days and nights, people have a party. They wear fun costumes. There are floats and parades of people playing the guitar, singing and dancing up and down the streets. And, of course, there is food everywhere! Celebration is in the air.

King Momo is the happy, fat king who rules the carnival cheerfully.

WHY IS THERE A CARNIVAL?

Every year, for forty days, Catholics observe a long period of fasting called Lent. During Lent, they don't eat meat or eggs or things made from milk. Lent ends with Easter Sunday, after which everything goes back to normal. People get together to have a great time before they begin fasting, and for three days they throw caution to the winds. This is the Carnival.

KING MOMO

King Momo is supposed to be the King of Carnivals in countries like Brazil, Colombia and Portugal, where the Carnival is also celebrated. Every year, a tall, fat man is chosen to be King Momo. He dresses up in magnificent robes and declares the Carnival open.

Hey, I would make a great King Momo.

FOOTBALL FEVER

Goans love football. And that's probably because the Portuguese brought it with them. In Goa, almost every village has its own team. And just like the IPL cricket matches, in football too there are teams. Goa's main teams are owned by business people.

The main football clubs are Dempo, Salgaocar, SESA Goa and Churchill Brothers. Oh, when there's a football match on, people go crazy, all right.

WEDDING TIME

Weddings in Goa are a mixed-up affair. There are fisherfolk who have their own traditions, the Catholics marry their own way, and the Hindus have their own traditions too! There are fun rituals with one thing in common. There is always lots of music, dance and drinks.

TRA LA LA LA

Goans really do have music in their blood. Thanks to the Portuguese, people learned Western instruments like the piano and the guitar. Many musicians moved out of Goa and started bands of their own. Some of Goa's famous musicians are Mickey Correa, Chic Chocolate and Johnny Baptist. You must have heard of Remo Fernandes too!

Remo Fernandes is one of Goa's most famous singers and composers. He sings, writes and plays the guitar and flute. He has also composed lots of songs for Hindi movies.

Wow!

WHAT'S ODD?

There's one word that doesn't fit in each row. Can you circle it?

DEMPO   SALGAOCAR   SESA GOA   MANCHESTER UNITED

MICKEY CORREA   CHIC CHOCOLATE   MICHAEL JACKSON   REMO FERNANDES

KING MOMO   KING ARTHUR   KING AKBAR   JULIUS CAESAR

EASTER   DIWALI   EID   MOTHER'S DAY

Bricks and stones

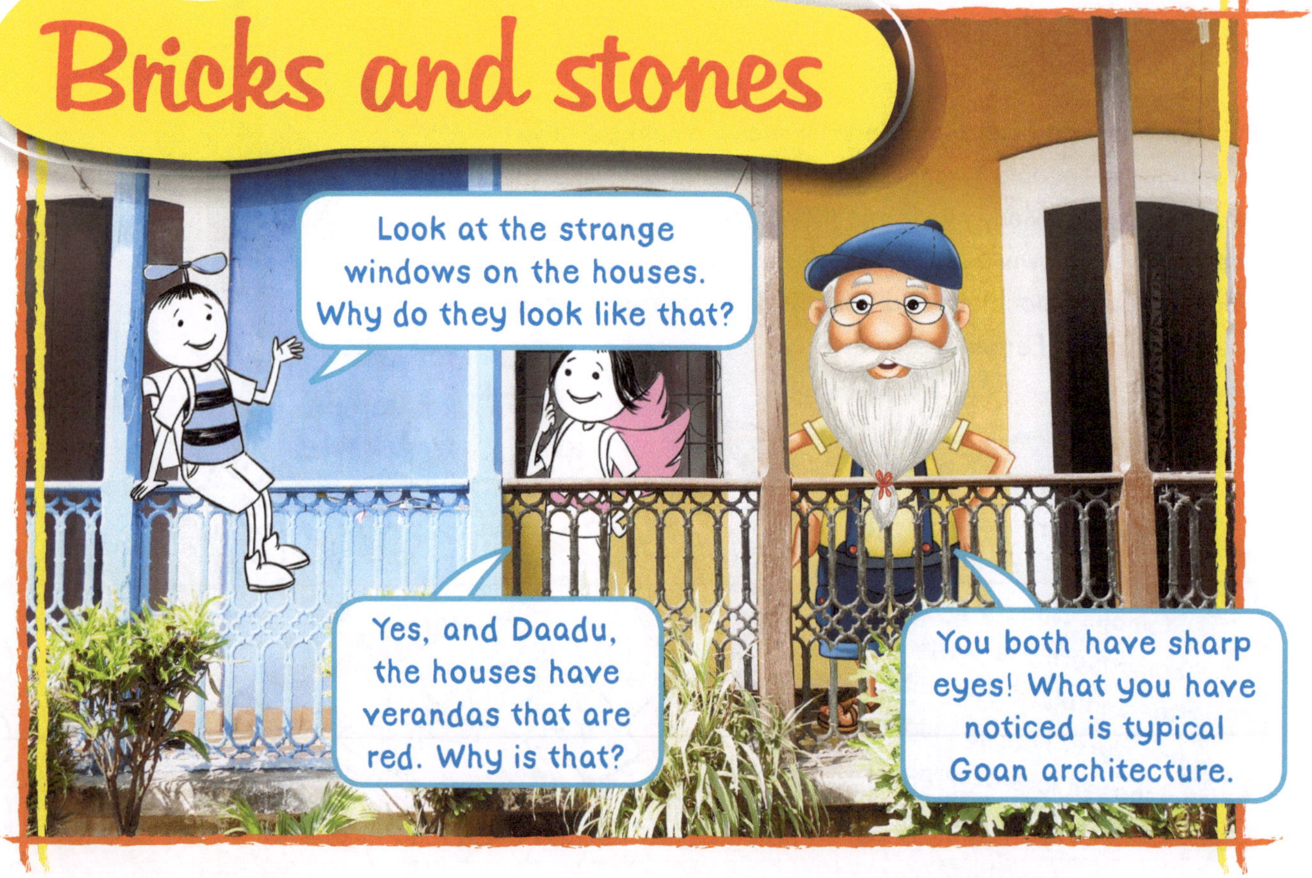

Look at the strange windows on the houses. Why do they look like that?

Yes, and Daadu, the houses have verandas that are red. Why is that?

You both have sharp eyes! What you have noticed is typical Goan architecture.

HOME SWEET HOME

Before the Portuguese arrived in Goa, people built houses that were mainly made of mud and had thatched roofs. There was always a courtyard right at the centre, in which the family would spend time together and eat their meals. These houses had tiny windows. The people who built these were mainly fisherfolk and farmers.

COLOURED SPLENDOUR

Soon the Portuguese arrived. And with them came a new style of architecture. They built big, big mansions. They painted these in sunny yellows and bright blues. They built long balconies in the front where the family would relax together.

A STRICT NO TO WHITE!

People say that for a long time, there was a rule in Portuguese occupied Goa: *no house could be painted white.* Only churches and chapels were allowed to be white. But if a house was left unpainted, the owner had to pay a big, fat fine.

Oops! That's quite a problem to have.

FONTAINHAS

When you go to this part of Goa, you feel as if you have gone back a few hundred years in time in Portugal. It has narrow streets with colourful houses. It used to have many springs and fountains and that is where it gets its name from.

WINDOW DRESSING

In many old Goan houses you will see unusual windows. Instead of glass, they are made of flat shells that are found on the beaches. These windows allow light to come in while also keeping a room cool from the hot, Goan sun.

Windows made of seashells

HAVE A SEAT

When the Goans built houses, they made sure they had enough space in which they could just chill. You will see that many old homes in Goa have a red stone bench that is built into the wall. This tells us that Goans are a friendly lot. The men and women of the house would sit around these benches, meet people passing by and chat with neighbours.

What a lovely house!

COLOURFUL GLASS

Thanks to the European influence that the Portuguese brought with them, many homes in Goa have beautiful stained glass on top of the windows.

Do It Yourself
Stained Glass Window

1 Draw different shapes on a cardboard window and cut them out carefully.

2 Paste pieces of different coloured cellophane paper behind the cutout shapes.

3 Hold the cardboard against the sun and see some lovely colours shining through.

Voila! You have a lovely stained glass window.

Standing strong

Daadu Dolma, there are so many different types of monuments here. Why are they so different from each other?

You see, Pushka, the monuments in Goa tell us the story of Goa's 1000 year history.

Oh, I see!

FANTASTIC FORTS

Goa has many forts. That is because the Portuguese and the various kings before them had to fight many wars. They tried to protect themselves by building forts so they could stop armies from attacking.

AGUADA FORT

This beautiful fort was built more than 400 years ago. That's OLD! It is Goa's largest fort. It was built to guard the entrance of River Mandovi. It has a tall lighthouse right in its centre that showed sailors the way. In the earlier days, fresh water springs flowed from this spot. When ships came from Portugal, tired sailors refreshed themselves with clean water here.

Fort Aguada is a prison today!

OOOH! SCARY!

REIS MAGOS FORT

The Portuguese decided they had to guard River Mandovi extra carefully. They built another fort called the Reis Magos Fort a little further away from Fort Aguada. Over the years, they kept making it larger and larger. They made sure it was defended by thirty-three guns and had enough space for soldiers to live. Like everywhere else, here too they built a beautiful church. After the Portuguese left Goa, for many years it was used as a prison. Now, it is just a monument that people love to visit.

TEREKHOL FORT

This fort was built by the Raja of Sawantwadi. Some years later, the Portuguese captured it. They built a chapel in it too. When the local Goans began to fight the Portuguese to leave them alone, a revolt was led from this fort.

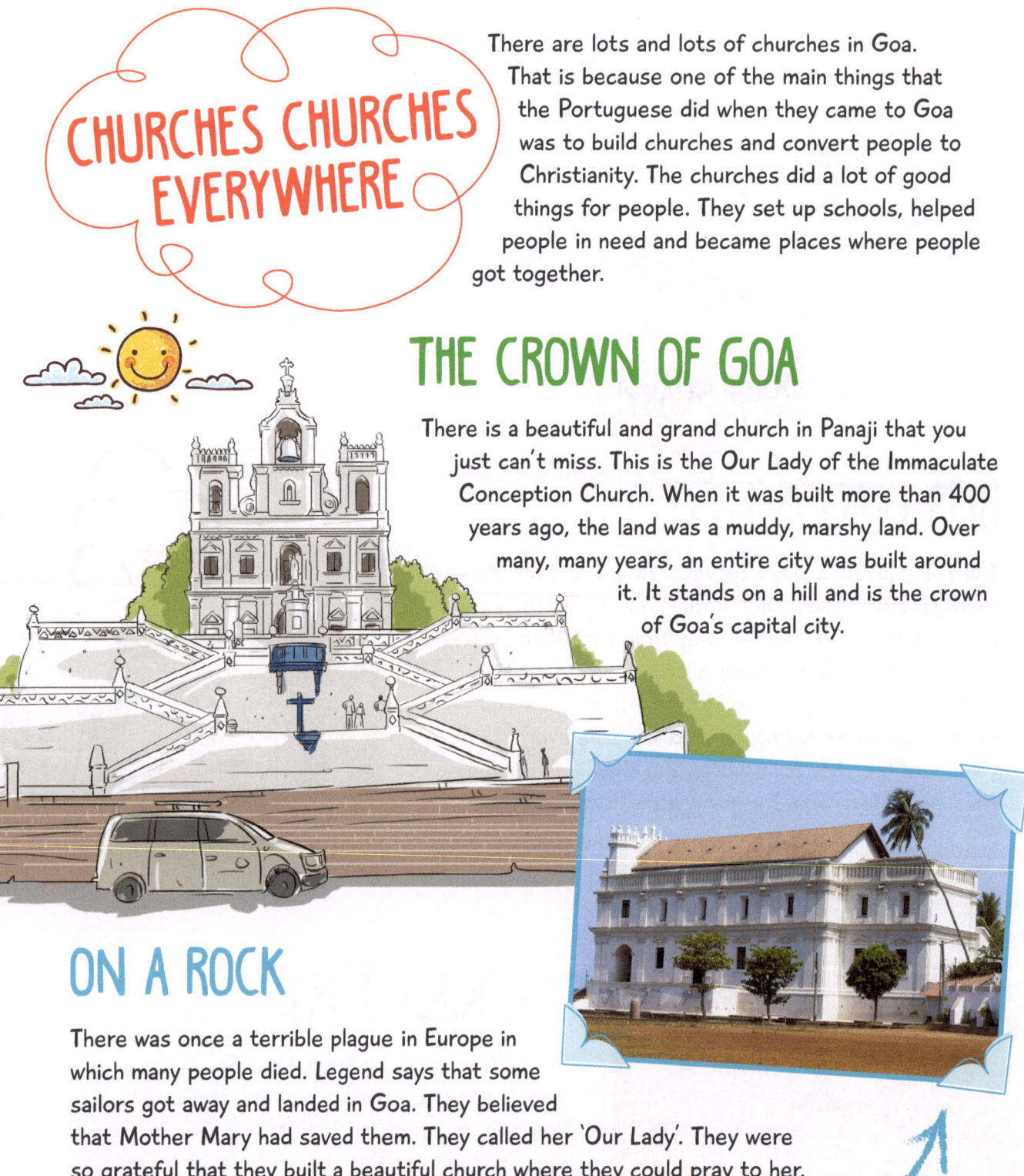

CHURCHES CHURCHES EVERYWHERE

There are lots and lots of churches in Goa. That is because one of the main things that the Portuguese did when they came to Goa was to build churches and convert people to Christianity. The churches did a lot of good things for people. They set up schools, helped people in need and became places where people got together.

THE CROWN OF GOA

There is a beautiful and grand church in Panaji that you just can't miss. This is the Our Lady of the Immaculate Conception Church. When it was built more than 400 years ago, the land was a muddy, marshy land. Over many, many years, an entire city was built around it. It stands on a hill and is the crown of Goa's capital city.

ON A ROCK

There was once a terrible plague in Europe in which many people died. Legend says that some sailors got away and landed in Goa. They believed that Mother Mary had saved them. They called her 'Our Lady'. They were so grateful that they built a beautiful church where they could pray to her. They called it the Church of Our Lady of the Rock of France.

THE MOST FAMOUS OF THEM ALL

The Bom Jesus Basilica is probably Goa's most famous church. People from all over the world come here to pray. Like many other churches, this one is over 400 years old. This is where St Francis Xavier's body was kept for many years for his followers to pray to. Even now, there is a beautiful statue of St Francis Xavier.

400-year-old church!

JUMBLED UP

Unscramble the mixed-up words in red and find the names of these famous churches in Goa.

1. Bom SUSEJ Basilica

2. Church of St CISNARF of Assisi

3. Church of Our YDAL of the Immaculate Conception

4. LEPAHC of St Catherine

5. Church of Lady of YRASOR

6. Chapel of St Francis REIVAX

7. Church of Our Lady of SELCARIM

Clue: Try spelling them backwards.

There are as many temples in Goa as there are churches. As we know, this is because till the Portuguese came, Goa was populated with Hindus. The main room of the temple is where the deity is placed. Around this, there is always a passage so that people can pray to God from all sides.

Seven-storeys-high lamp tower

MANGESHI TEMPLE

The Mangeshi Temple, which is dedicated to Lord Shiva, is one of Goa's most beautiful temples. In the courtyard of the temple, there is a beautiful lamp tower that is almost seven storeys high. Wow! There is also a statue of a Nandi Bull (the animal that Lord Shiva rode) right at the entrance.

SHANTADURGA TEMPLE

Once, Lord Shiva and Lord Vishnu got into a fight. Lord Shiva's wife, Parvati, took the form of a woman called Shantadurga. She stood between them to stop the fight. The Shantadurga Temple is dedicated to her. Her idol has a snake on either side. These two snakes represent Lord Shiva and Lord Vishnu.

THE MAHALAXMI TEMPLE

When the Portuguese arrived, the Hindus got worried. They built the Mahalaxmi Temple (Mahalaxmi is the goddess of peace). It has beautiful domes and the walls are decorated with pictures and carvings of Hanuman—the monkey God.

The story of Lord Krishna is told through pictures on panels.

JUMBLED WORDS

Can you find the names of these famous Goan temples hidden in this grid?
Mangeshi; Nageshi; Vijayadurga; Shantadurga; Mahadev; Mahalaxmi

A	D	R	N	F	E	D	C	B	A	M
V	I	J	A	Y	A	D	U	R	G	A
M	A	N	G	E	S	H	I	O	K	H
W	R	T	E	U	I	R	T	H	J	A
O	P	V	S	T	G	E	H	E	H	D
I	M	A	H	A	L	A	X	M	I	E
C	W	M	I	S	J	M	K	J	K	V
S	H	A	N	T	A	D	U	R	G	A

OLD GOA

Ruins of Church of St Augustine →

A TREASURE OF HISTORY

There are lots of ancient monuments in a part called Old Goa. Even before the Portuguese arrived, this was a beautiful city. It was the second capital of the sultans of Bijapur. This area has lots of mosques, temples, forts and churches as well. Many of these are so old and precious that UNESCO decided to declare Old Goa a World Heritage Site.

Did you know?
World Heritage Sites are the most precious places in the world where human history is saved.

THE VICEROY'S ARCH

When Vasco da Gama discovered the sea route from Portugal to India, there was a lot of excitement. Years later, his grandson Francesco da Gama was sent to Goa as the viceroy (who is a sort of head of a state). He built a beautiful arch made of deep black stone. Every time there was a new viceroy, something new was carved on the stone.

Francesco must have been so proud of his grandad!!

GATE OF THE FORTRESS OF ADIL SHAH

During the Muslim rule, King Adil Shah built a magnificent fort. After the Muslim rule ended, the fort was abandoned and it fell to ruin. All that was left was a beautiful entrance.

Close your eyes and you can imagine horses thundering through these gates.

BLOCKY PUZZLE

Help Mishki fill in all the squares. In the orange squares you will find a word which means something that is an entranceway.

The fortress gate of _____ Shah.

The broken down state of the fortress means

it is in _____

St Augustine is a _____

UNESCO has declared Old Goa a World _____ Site.

Working hard

Daadu, what do the people of Goa do?

Well, there are fisherfolk, farmers and business people as well.

And because so many people from all over the world come to Goa, there are lots of hotels and shops too.

LET'S GO FISHING

Goans just LOVE fish. With sea surrounding the state, fishing is something they have been doing for centuries. One of Goa's fishing communities is called the Kharvi. These are simple fisherfolk who earn their living by catching and selling fish. Every day, the menfolk go off to the sea—often in groups of twenty or twenty-five. The women sell the fish in one of the many, many fishmarkets around Goa.

Fishermen at work

FARMER, FARMER, WHAT DO YOU GROW?

After fishing, farming is the next biggest occupation. There are many beautiful emerald-green fields in which farmers grow crops. During the rains, they grow lots of rice. After that, the farmers grow pulses and millets. There are many fruit orchards too, where cashews, papayas, mangoes, bananas and jackfruit are grown.

NUTS FOR COCONUTS

Of course! So many coconut trees around tell us that people grow and use lots of coconuts too! There are many, many coconut plantations and Goans sell coconut as well as things made of coconut.

FISHY TANGLE

This fish is trying to escape the fisherman's net. Can you help it get away?

MARKET MADNESS

Mishki and Pushka have gone shopping to the busy Goan market.

Find twenty differences in the two pictures given here.

What a busy, busy market!

Yum yum yum . . .

Daadu Dolma, I'm hungreeeee. What can we eat in Goa?

You're lucky, Mishki. Goa has some amazing food. Come, I'll tell you all about some of Goa's most special dishes.

A TASTY MIXED BAG

Thanks to the Portuguese and all the other invaders who came and lived in Goa for hundreds of years, Goan food is a yummy mix of Indian and Western fare. For their main lunch and dinner, rice and curry is a favourite. Of course, fish is almost always there for meals.

Goans use lots of coconut in all their food.

Yummy fish curry

CURRY IN A HURRY

These are the yummiest curries in Goa. Because there are so many coconut trees, many curries are made of coconut. And then people add fish, prawns, crabs and even meat to the curries. One famous curry is the Xacuti curry.

Did you know?
Xacuti is pronounced as Shacuti.

FROM PORTUGAL WITH LOVE

The Portuguese brought some amazing recipes with them. Sorpotel is a sour and spicy dish with meat. Vindaloo is another dish that is very spicy with a red, thick curry.

Vindaloo

Sorpotel

What a feast!!!

Looks yummy!!

SO SWEET!

Like all of us, Goans love sweets. And they sure have a lot of them for Christmas, weddings and other feasts. There are many types of sweets, but two of them simply **HAVE** to be eaten.

Bibinca is a sweet made of coconut milk, jaggery, butter and flour. It's not easy to make. It's made in many, many layers that you see when you slice it.

Dodol sounds funny but tastes yummy. It's a soft, gooey sweet that you can cut into tiny squares and pop into your mouth!

Bibinca

Dodol

KAJU FENI

Now here's a drink children should **NOT** have, but grown-up Goans love. It is made of the juice of the kaju fruit. The juice is fermented and kept for days and days in barrels. But not everyone likes the taste.

Mishki, the bibinca and dodol are so tempting!

Hmm . . . but children should never try feni. Remember that!

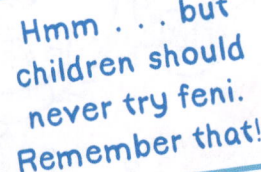

THE POEM OF GOA

Mishki has written a lovely poem about Goa. But she has got her words mixed up. Help her complete the rhyme.

Goa is such a lovely state
Go and visit it, just don't _____

It has lovely beaches and friendly people
And churches galore, with spires and _____

And oh! The food, it is so yummy
I ate so much, it filled my _____

The farmers are busy putting rice in the hatch
And fishermen are busy pulling in their _____

The rivers are full of boats and ferries
With people going across or just making _____

Listen now to the temple bells
Then go and see what the fisherwoman _____

The lovely Goan dances and the beautiful songs
You will just want to sing and dance _____

You'll love Goa in the sun or the rain,
You'll want to go there again and _____

What to wear?

Isn't Goa colourful? And see, women are wearing different types of clothes.

Again, it's thanks to the Portuguese. We've seen that Goan history is different from any other state in India. And that's what makes everything different about it. Even clothes.

DRESSED FOR FISHING

Fishermen wear bright shirts with a loincloth wrapped around their lower body. Modern fishermen just wear shorts. The fisherwomen wear a sari that is wrapped tight and high to make it easy for them to move.

NAUVARI SARI

Many traditional women wear a long, long sari, which is nine yards long. It is called a nauvari sari.

DRESSED TO THE HILT

Men in Goa dress in normal western clothes: shirts, trousers and jackets. But when it's party time (which it often is in Goa), they are dressed to the hilt.

PANO-BHAJU

This is a dress that is a mix of East and West. The lower part is like a sari or a lungi. And the upper part is like a blouse that women wore in Portugal. It has heavy gold embroidery that the Mughal kings had on their clothes. See how many traditions are all mixed up? Women wear it now during Mando—a lovely song and dance.

SKIRTS AND GOWNS

Ah! The Portuguese are back with their dresses. Many Goan Catholic women wear long skirts or dresses. They also wear gowns for balls, dances and weddings.

Autograph, please?

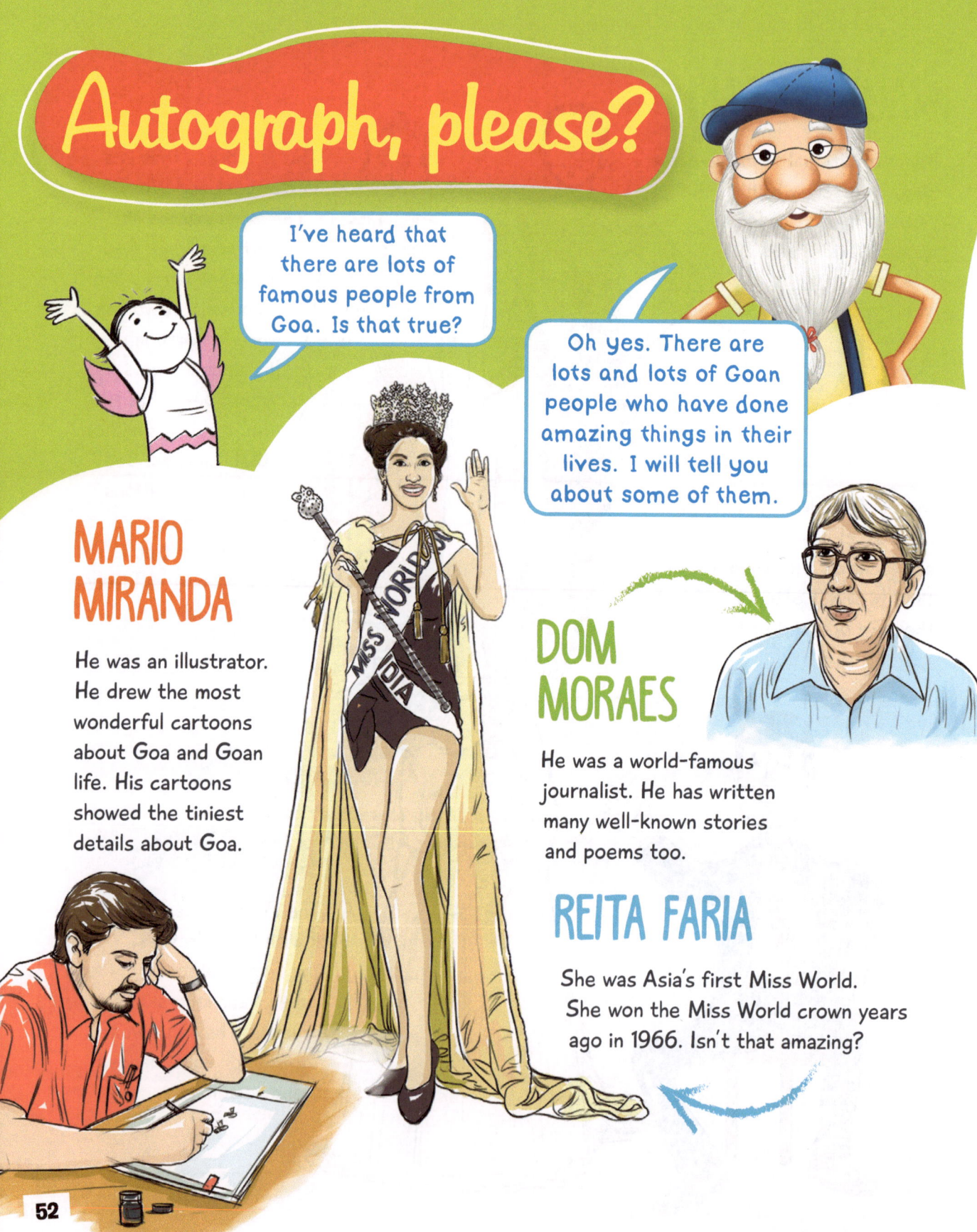

I've heard that there are lots of famous people from Goa. Is that true?

Oh yes. There are lots and lots of Goan people who have done amazing things in their lives. I will tell you about some of them.

MARIO MIRANDA

He was an illustrator. He drew the most wonderful cartoons about Goa and Goan life. His cartoons showed the tiniest details about Goa.

DOM MORAES

He was a world-famous journalist. He has written many well-known stories and poems too.

REITA FARIA

She was Asia's first Miss World. She won the Miss World crown years ago in 1966. Isn't that amazing?

LATA MANGESHKAR

She holds a world record for the most number of songs sung in Indian languages. She is called the Nightingale of India.

LEANDER PAES

He is a tennis player who has won many, many Grand Slam titles.

KISHORI AMONKAR

She was one of India's greatest classical singers. She received awards such as the Padma Bhushan and Padma Vibhushan.

WENDELL RODRICKS

He is a well-known fashion designer who designs clothes for film stars and celebrities.

WORD WHEEL

Can you help Mishki make small words out of the letters in the wheel? You must make at least one word using all the letters. And that word is the name of a famous person from Goa.

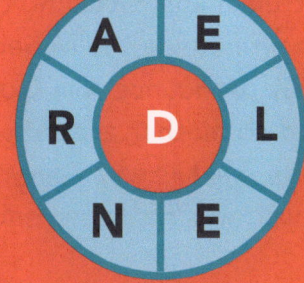

A E R D L N E

Once upon a time . . .

Now, Daadu Dolma, tell us a story from Goa.

That's a great idea. Goa has lots and lots of folk tales and stories. I will tell you one of them.

THE STORY OF ATTULEM AND BITTULEM

Once upon a time, there were two sisters whose names were Attulem and Bittulem. (You don't have to pronounce the M because that's how they pronounce it in Goa.) Attulem and Bittulem had no mother and father, but they were happy and kind little girls. That is why everyone loved them and looked after them. Their tiny house was near a forest. They loved animals and animals loved them back.

The squirrels would bring them crunchy nuts to eat. The monkeys would bring them juicy mangoes to suck on. The bats would bring them sweet and sour guavas. And the elephants would bring them firewood to keep them warm on cold nights.

Now there was an evil tiger called Vaag Maam who didn't like that the animals were so good to the girls. He wanted the animals to do everything only for him. He became very jealous of the girls.

One day, he sniffed here and he sniffed there.

'Who is cooking sorpotel?' he roared. 'It is my favourite food.'

He saw that the animals had cooked yummy sorpotel and were taking it for Attulem and Bittulem.

He thought hard. 'I will eat up Attulem and Bittulem and stop this nonsense once and for all. And I will get all the sorpotel too!' He crept up to the house of Attulem and Bittulem. The animals saw him and began to shout loudly to warn the two girls.

Attulem and Bittulem trembled in fear when they heard the roar. There were two large jars in the room filled with spices. Attulem jumped into one jar and Bittulem jumped into the other.

'Aaah!' said Vaag Maam. 'I will take these two jars and make some spicy sorpotel myself.'

He picked up the jars and began walking out. Just then, the spices in one of the jars tickled Attulem's nose.

'ACHOOOOOOOOOOO!' she sneezed loudly. The jar broke into a million pieces and the spices scattered in the air.

'What was that?' Vaag Maam jumped up in fright. The pieces of glass pierced his body like a thousand arrows.

'I am being attacked,' he yelled. He ran for his life. He ran out of the house, out of the jungle and out of Attulem and Bittulem's life.

The animals came out and rejoiced. And Attulem, Bittulem and all the animals lived happily ever after, without the horrible Vaag Maam to bother them.

TRAVEL DIARY

Have you enjoyed this trip to Goa with your friends Mishki and Pushka—and, of course, with Daadu Dolma?

Now you can make your own Goa diary. And if you ever visit Goa, make sure you take pictures and put them in the photo box.

The first place I would visit in Goa:

_____

If I ever meet Vasco da Gama, this is what I would say to him:

_____

The one Goan dish I am definitely going to eat:

_____

The fort I think is the most interesting:

_____

The one famous person from Goa I would love to meet:

_____

If I were Portuguese, my name would be:

_____

The festival from Goa that I think is the most fun:

_____

The five words that I think describe Goa the best are:

_____

_____

_____

_____

_____

My Goa memories:

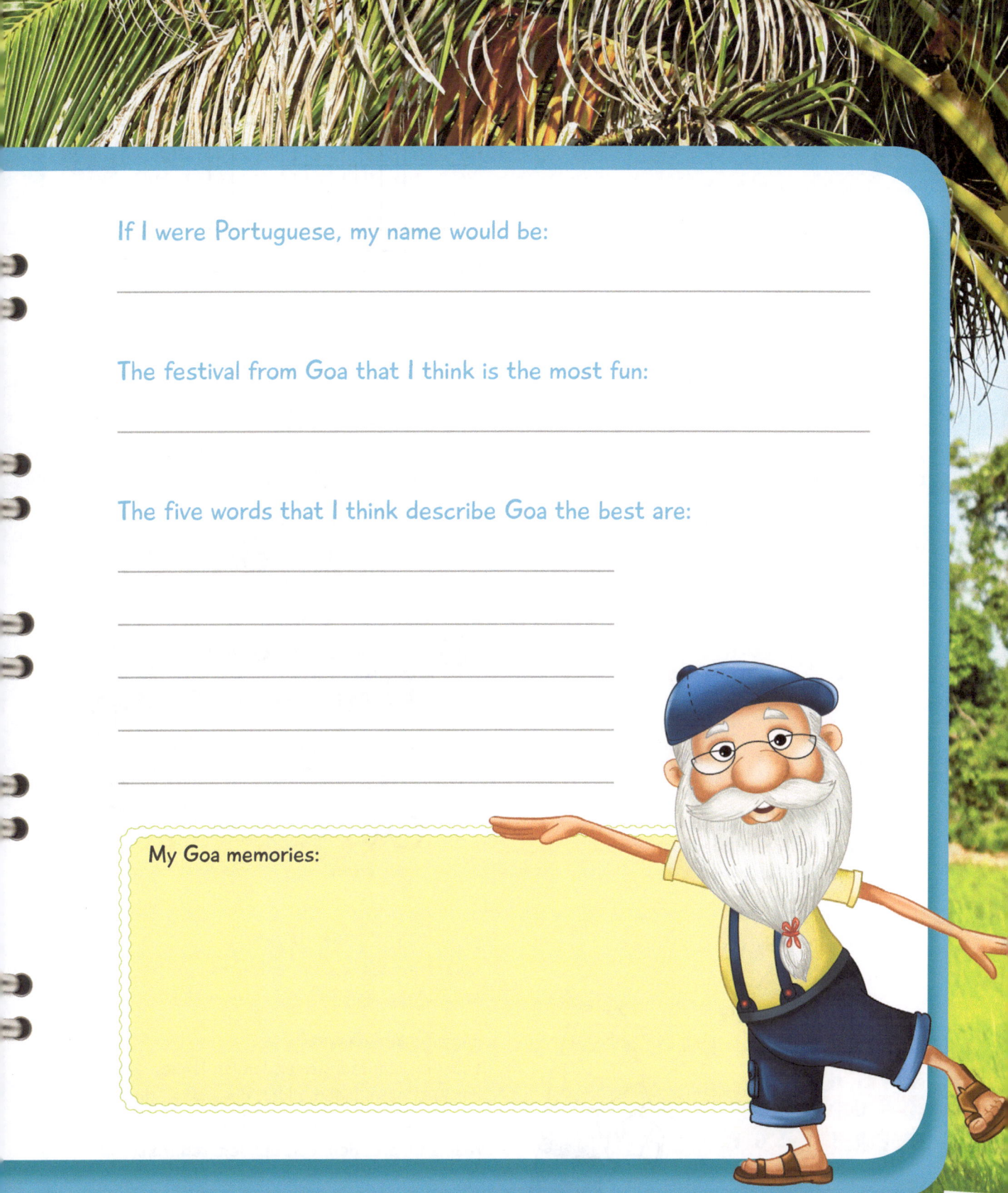

ANSWERS

page 9 MIXED-UP RIVERS
Mandovi, Zuari, Terekhol, Kushavati, Sal

page 16-17 LOST

page 19 CRACK THE CODE
GOA IS NOW A STATE.

page 21 MATCH THE WORDS
Where - Khayee, Child - Chardu, I want - Maka zai, I don't want - Maka naka, Come - Yo, Thank you - Obrigaado, Water - Udak, Up - Vair

page 24 SHADOWPLAY

page 29 WHAT'S ODD?
Manchester United, Michael Jackson, King Momo, Mother's Day

page 37 JUMBLED UP
Jesus, Francis, Lady, Chapel, Rosary, Xavier, Miracles

page 41 BLOCKY PUZZLE
ADIL
RUINS
CHURCH
HERITAGE

page 39 JUMBLED WORDS

A	D	R	N	F	E	D	C	B	A	M
V	I	J	A	Y	A	D	U	R	G	A
M	A	N	G	E	S	H	I	O	K	H
W	R	T	E	U	I	R	T	H	J	A
O	P	V	S	T	G	E	H	E	H	D
I	M	A	H	A	L	A	X	M	I	E
C	W	M	I	S	J	M	K	J	K	V
S	H	A	N	T	A	D	U	R	G	A

page 43 FISHY TANGLE
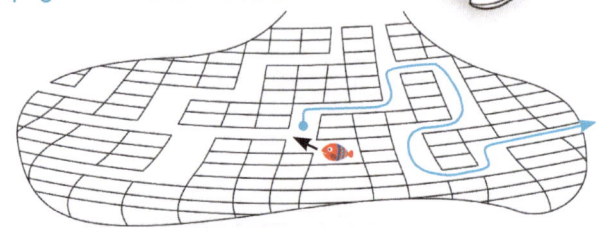

page 45 BUSY MARKET

page 49 THE POEM OF GOA
wait, steeples, tummy, catch, merry, sells, along, again

page 53 WORD WHEEL
Leander, learned, dealer, leader, lender, leaner, earned, learn, laden, elder, deer, dear, deal, dare, near, earn, land, lane, lead, need, read, real, and, are, den, ear, eel, led, red, ran, end